# The Big Day!
# Going to the Hospital

Nicola Barber

**PowerKiDS** press™

New York

Published in 2009 by The Rosen Publishing Group Inc.
29 East 21st Street, New York, NY 10010

First Edition

Editor: Camilla Lloyd
Designer: Elaine Wilkinson
Picture Researcher: Kathy Lockley

Library of Congress Cataloging-in-Publication Data

Barber, Nicola.
  Going to the hospital / Nicola Barber. — 1st ed.
      p. cm. — (The big day!)
  Includes index.
  ISBN 978-1-4358-2840-7 (library binding)
  ISBN 978-1-4358-2896-4 (paperback)
  ISBN 978-1-4358-2901-5 (6-pack)
  1. Children—Preparation for medical care—Juvenile literature.  I. Title.
  R130.5.B37 2009
  362.11—dc22

                                    2008025812

Manufactured in China

Picture Acknowledgments: The author and publisher would like to thank the following for their
pictures to be reproduced in this publication: Cover photograph: LWA-JDC/Corbis; Charles
Thatcher/Stone/Getty Images: 7; Colin Gray/Photonica/Getty Images: 21; Corbis: 16, 24;
Doable/Acollection/Getty Images: 20; Duncan Raban/Great Ormond Street Hospital for
Children: 8, 13; Great Ormond Street Hospital for Children: 11; Janine Wiedel Photo
Library/Alamy Images: 15; Jeff Kaufman/Taxi/Getty Images: 6; Jennie Woodcock/Bubbles
Photolibrary: 17; John Birdsall/John Birdsall Social Issues Photo Library: 9, 19; LWA-
JDC/Corbis: 18; Peter Dazeley/Photographer's Choice/Getty Images: 14; Photofusion Picture
Library: 1, 12; Picture Partners/Alamy Images: 10; Randy Faris/Corbis: 5.

# Contents

Feeling unwell                             4

Seeing the doctor                          6

At the hospital                            8

Staying overnight                         10

Friends and playtime                      12

Finding out what's wrong                  14

Having an operation                       16

Visitors                                  18

Going home                                20

Hospital words                            22

Further information and Web Sites         23

Index                                     24

# Feeling unwell

It's not much fun feeling unwell.
When your throat is sore or your
head hurts, you don't feel like doing much.

**What happens when you don't feel well?**

When you are sick, you don't go to school.
You stay at home so that your Mom or
Dad can look after you.

# Seeing the doctor

Sometimes when you are sick, your parents take you to see a doctor. Usually, you go to see the doctor at the doctor's office.

But sometimes you might have to go
to the hospital to see a different doctor,
or to have some tests.

# At the hospital

Hospitals are often big and busy places, with lots of people. All the nurses and doctors wear tags with their names on.

You might only stay in the hospital for a few hours. If you have to stay for longer, you will be given a special bracelet with your name on it.

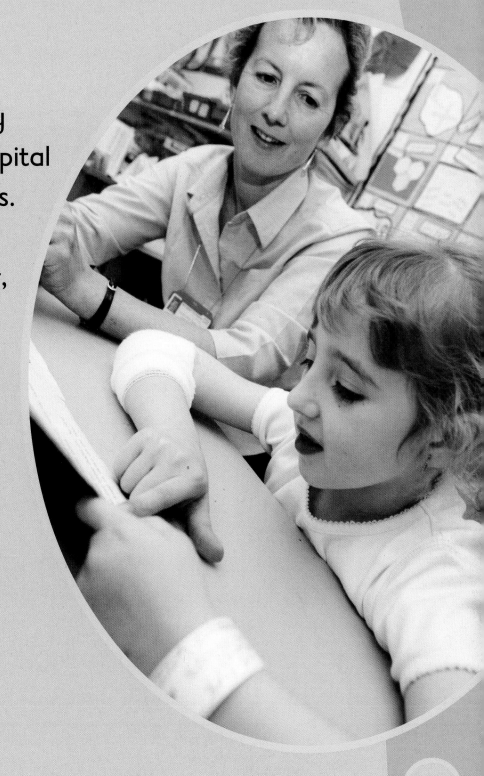

# Staying overnight

Sometimes you might need to stay in the hospital for a while.

If you are going to stay overnight, you will need to pack your pajamas, your toothbrush, and a special toy for company.

You could take a few of your favorite games or books. Usually, your Mom or Dad will stay in the hospital with you to help the nurses take care of you.

# Friends and playtime

A nurse will show you where your bed is. You might be in a room on your own, or you might be sharing a room with several other children. This is called a ward.

Most children's wards have a playroom,
full of toys and things to do. You can eat
your meals in the ward, and you might even
have your own TV by your bed.

# Finding out what's wrong

Hospitals have lots of equipment and machines to help doctors and nurses find out why you are sick. Some machines listen to your heart beating or measure your temperature.

Other machines take pictures of your bones. The doctor might need to take some of your blood to check it.

# Having an operation

You might need an operation to make you feel better. You will probably have to wear a special gown that closes at the back. You won't be able to have anything to eat or drink for a while before the operation—you'll probably feel hungry!

The doctor will give you a shot to make you sleep during the operation. Afterward, the nurse will tell you when you can start to drink and eat again.

# Visitors

Your family and friends can come to visit you while you are in the hospital.

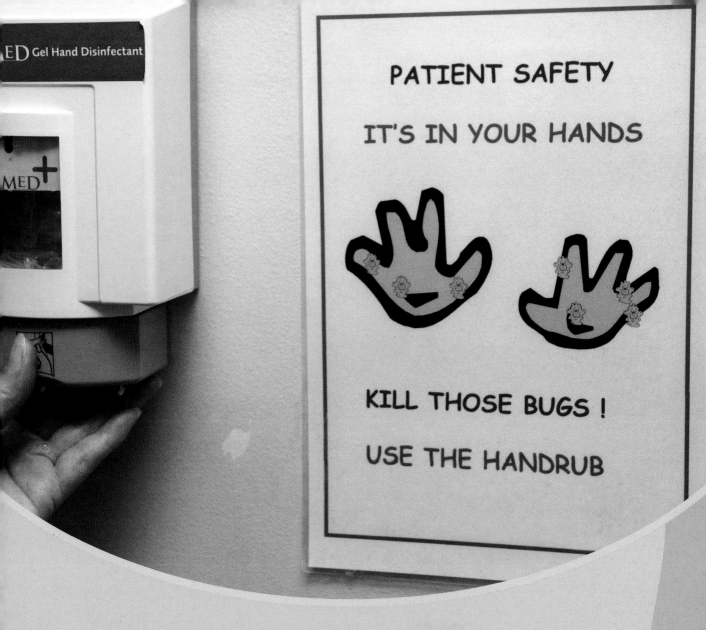

PATIENT SAFETY

IT'S IN YOUR HANDS

KILL THOSE BUGS !

USE THE HANDRUB

Before they come into the ward, everyone must wash their hands with special soap to make sure they are clean. Some wards have a doorbell, so a nurse can let people in.

# Going home

When you are well enough, it is time to go home. You can say goodbye to your friends at the hospital. Sometimes you will take some medicine home with you.

Later, you might need to go back to the hospital for a short visit, so the doctor can check that you are completely better.

**Get well soon!**

# Hospital words

If you are writing about going to the hospital, these are some words you might need to use.

Blood

Operation

Bracelet

Shot

Doctor

Sick

Doctor's office

Tag

Gown

Temperature

Medicine

Nurse

Ward

# Further information

## Books

**Going to the Hospital (Usborne First Experiences)**
by Michelle Bates (Usborne Books, 2005)

**The Hospital**
by Debbie Bailey (Annick Press, 2000)

## Web Sites

Due to the changing nature of Internet links, PowerKids Press has developed an online list of Web sites related to the subject of this book. This site is updated regularly. Please use this link to access this list:
www.powerkidslinks.com/bd/hospital

# Index

**B**

bed 12, 13
blood 15
bones 15

**D**

Dad 5, 11
doctor 6, 7, 8, 14, 15,
    17, 21
doctor's office 6

**F**

feeling sick 4, 5, 6, 14

**H**

hospital 7, 8, 9, 10, 11,
    14, 18, 20, 21
hospital bracelet 9
hospital gown 16

**M**

machines 14, 15
meals 13
medicine 20
Mom 5, 11

**N**

name tags 8
nurse 8, 11, 12, 14,
    17, 19

**O**

operation 16, 17

**P**

playroom 13

**S**

shot 17

**T**

temperature 5, 14
tests 7
toys 10, 13

**V**

visitors 18, 19

**W**

ward 12, 13, 19
washing 19